Pope John Paul II

Pope John Paul II

Patricia Cronin Marcello

Ariel Books

**Andrews McMeel
Publishing**

Kansas City

www.andrewsmcmeel.com

ISBN: 0-8362-7160-2
Library of Congress Catalog Card Number: 98-85420

Contents

Introduction

Pope John Paul II, spiritual leader of the Roman Catholic Church since 1978, may be one of the most controversial pontiffs in history, but he is also one of the most beloved. His humanity, intellectualism, and unwavering faith are greatly admired both inside and outside the church. The hardships he endured early in his life (his mother and older brother died while he was still a child, and

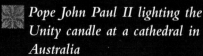 *Pope John Paul II lighting the Unity candle at a cathedral in Australia*

his homeland was invaded by Germany just as he came to manhood) only served to deepen his courage, his great love of God, and his respect for human life.

When Karol Wojtyla was elected pope, many believed he would bring a liberal outlook to the church. This, however, has not been the case. Pope John Paul II's conservative views on matters such as women in the church, homosexuality, premarital sex, contra-

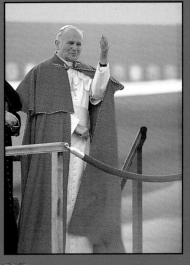

The pope arriving in one of many countries he has visited

Pope John Paul II receiving flowers when visiting the United States

ception, and abortion have disappointed many and resulted in strong criticism from people around the world. But few can fail to admire John Paul's enormous strength of character, his unquestionable faith, and his empathy and love for the downtrodden of the world. He has worked tirelessly for world peace, traveling around the globe to bring his message directly to the tens of thousands of people who have gathered to hear him. He was instrumental in the fall of communism in Poland and elsewhere, and he established the Vatican as an important voice in world affairs. John Paul is an ecumenist who strives to bring all faiths together in love and understanding. Statesman, moral leader, campaigner for peace, champion of the poor—Pope John Paul's message of love, faith, and hope transcends present-day controversies and makes him one of the most influential men of our times.

The Road to the Vatican

On May 18, 1920, Karol Jozef Wojtyla (pronounced Voy-tee-wah) was born in Wadowice, Poland. His father, Carolus, was an administrative officer in the Polish army. His mother, Emilia, loved him as only a mother who has lost an earlier child can (Karol's infant sister, Olga, had died six years before his birth). She called him "Lolek," a diminutive of Karol, and would often say, "My Lolek will become a great person."

Three pregnancies had adversely affected Emilia's health, and when Karol was only four weeks from his ninth birthday, she succumbed to an inflammation of the heart and kidneys. Utterly devastated by his loss, Karol found comfort in his deepening relationship with his brother Edmund. Edmund was fourteen years older, but he loved his little brother, and they spent a great deal of Edmund's free time hiking and playing soccer together. But tragedy

Karol Wojtyla as a boy in his school uniform

struck yet again. Edmund, who was a resident doctor at the Children's Clinic of Kraków, contracted scarlet fever from a patient and died in December 1932.

Mounting grief sent Karol toward books, schoolwork, and sports. From his father he soaked up Polish history and the German language. His first piece of writing was published in a church newspaper at age thirteen. At fourteen he discovered the theater and acting, to which he would dedicate many years of his life.

✳

After high school Karol attended Jagiellonian University in Kraków, but the university closed when the Nazis invaded Poland and World War II began. The Nazis ordered compulsory work for all adult Poles, sending many young men to Germany to perform forced labor for the Reich. To avoid exile or imprisonment, Karol managed to find a job

Karol, age twenty-six, outside the Solvay Chemical Plant

with the Solvay chemical company at Zakrzowek. There, he worked in the stone quarry eight hours a day in frigid temperatures, laying tracks, breaking rocks, setting blasting charges, and working in the factory.

※

There was still more tragedy to come for Karol: His father died in 1941. Karol channeled his seemingly never-ending grief into producing plays, prose, and poetry. That summer he became active in the underground

Rhapsodic Theater, which produced inspiring plays designed to rekindle the spirits of the oppressed people of Poland.

About a year later, Karol, who had always had a special relationship with God, heard His call. He was accepted into the archbishop of Kraków's underground seminary, established to protect students from Nazi persecution. In March 1943, under surveillance by the gestapo, Karol was

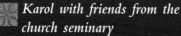

Karol with friends from the church seminary

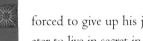

forced to give up his job and the theater to live in secret in the archbishop's
palace.

When the difficult war finally ended,
Jagiellonian University reopened, and
Karol resumed his studies. In only a
few months he joined the faculty as
an assistant instructor of theology.
He asked to become a Carmelite
father, but Archbishop Sapieha
refused to allow Karol's charisma and
brilliance to be shut behind

Karol as a young priest in 1945

monastery doors. Karol finally abandoned the idea of cloistered life, and he was ordained a priest in Sapieha's private chapel on November 1, 1946.

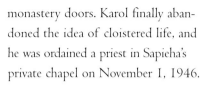

On November 26 he registered at the Angelicum University in Rome for postgraduate work. His doctoral dissertation was accepted in June 1948, but because of a rule stating that doctoral dissertations had to be printed, the degree could not be awarded. Father Wojtyla did not have the money to print the dissertation.

❉

He returned to Kraków and took the master's level exams at Jagiellonian University. He received top grades, was awarded the master's degree, and in less than two months earned the doctorate in Sacred Theology that had eluded him in Rome.

❉

During the same period he served as a parish priest in Niegowic, after which he was made vicar, or assistant

Karol (center) with other deacons in 1948

pastor, of St. Florian's Church in Kraków. Later, he became a full professor and chair of the ethics department at Catholic University in Lublin. From there, he became auxiliary bishop and then archbishop of Krakow.

Because of his good works on behalf of the church and the Polish people and his noteworthy participation in Vatican II in Rome, Pope Paul VI appointed Archbishop Wojtyla to the college of cardinals in 1967. Paul admired Wojtyla and often invited him to visit the papal apartments; it was obvious that Paul was preparing Wojtyla for the future.

＊

But Wojtyla was more than Paul's protégé. He was active in many areas. He was president of the Episcopal Conference in 1969, was elected to the secretary-general's council for the Synod of Bishops in 1971 and 1977, convoked the First National

Assembly of Physicians and Theologians in 1975, and at the request of Pope Paul VI, presented the spiritual exercise "Meditations" at the Vatican in 1976 (which was published as *A Sign of Contradiction* in 1979).

When Paul died, Albino Luciani became Pope John Paul I. Unfortunately, he died only thirty-three days after his election. Not many knew the name Karol Wojtyla then, but the new conclave realized that the church needed a leader with dynamic energy, inspiring faith, and strong pastoral skills. Karol Wojtyla became a top candidate, and would soon be known throughout the world as Pope John Paul II.

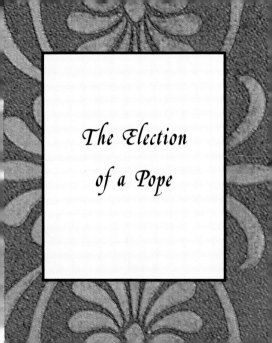

The Election of a Pope

The pope is the supreme ruler of the Roman Catholic Church and all of its followers. His reign continues until death. Up to 120 members of the sacred college of cardinals, who are the pope's counselors and assistants, form the "conclave," the body that elects a pope.

＊

When a pope dies, the election must begin no sooner than fifteen but not later than twenty days after his death. The conclaves are bound to absolute

A member of the Swiss guard at
one of the gates to the Vatican

secrecy. The cardinals are locked in the Sistine Chapel from the time the conclave begins until a pope is elected. At the start of the conclave, the cardinals take a vow to maintain absolute secrecy. This oath is strictly enforced and has been made more stringent in light of modern technology. Participants are not permitted televisions, radios, telephones, tape recorders, copiers, newspapers, or magazines. To enforce the rules in future conclaves, cardinals' residences

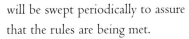

will be swept periodically to assure
that the rules are being met.

Voting begins on the afternoon of
the conclave's first day. Any Catholic
male may be elected, although all
popes since 1378 have been cardinals. Balloting continues until a candidate receives a two-thirds majority,
although a new rule states that if
the number of unsuccessful ballots
reaches thirty, a simple majority vote
will be accepted.

*Crowds in St. Peter's Square await
the election of a new pope in 1978*

When ballots are unsuccessful, the voting slips are burned with humid straw and chemicals. This makes black smoke, which arises from a chimney outside the Sistine Chapel and serves as a negative signal to the throngs of Vatican-watchers waiting in St. Peter's Square below, who know that if white smoke arises, a new pope has been chosen.

When a candidate receives the neces-

*A puff of white smoke announces
the election of John Paul II*

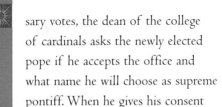

sary votes, the dean of the college of cardinals asks the newly elected pope if he accepts the office and what name he will choose as supreme pontiff. When he gives his consent and chooses a name, the conclave is officially over.

※

Karol Wojtyla was elected on October 16, 1978, after only eight ballots. He was the 264th true pope since St. Peter, the first pope, took the reins of the church from Jesus Christ. At

The procession during the coronation of Pope John Paul II

fifty-eight, he was the youngest pope since 1846, the first non-Italian pope in 456 years (since Pope Adrian VI in 1522), and the first-ever Polish pope.

Daily Life

Although the pope is surrounded by masterpieces of art and architecture at the Vatican, his daily life is simple. His room on the third floor of the Apostolic Palace overlooks St. Peter's Square. A single bed, a desk, and two straight-backed upholstered chairs are the only furniture. The parquet floor is bare except for a small rug, and the walls hold only a few Polish icons.

The pope begins his day at 5:30 A.M.

and by 6:15 he is praying in his private chapel. A bronze crucifix hangs over the altar, and an icon of Poland's precious Black Madonna of Czestochowa is close by. The priedieu, or kneeling bench, has a padded armrest that lifts up like a desk lid, under which the pope keeps prayer books and a thick stack of prayer intentions.

At 7:00 A.M. the pope says Mass, and afterward he breakfasts with

The pope celebrating Mass with Cardinal Hume

 The pope greeting children among a crowd of well-wishers

invited guests, which may include seminarians, Polish friends, or politicians. He uses mealtimes to discuss ideas of liturgy and policy with people from all walks of life, and he takes these opinions and ideas into consideration in his administration of the church.

A prolific writer since his youth, Pope John Paul II includes time for writing in his daily routine. Even now, his literary output is enormous,

and his letters, sermons, and speeches alone fill nearly 150 volumes. His book, *Crossing the Threshold of Hope,* was published in 1994. In 1997 one of his plays *(Our God's Brother)* was adapted for a movie and presented at the Venice Film Festival.

After he has spent about an hour writing, John Paul holds private and general audiences for the rest of the morning. Some of his well-known guests have been President and Mrs.

The pope visiting with Queen Elizabeth in 1982

Clinton, Lech Walesa, Mikhail Gorbachev, and Queen Elizabeth II.

✳

John Paul's guests at lunch are usually bishops. The meal may be pasta or antipasto, followed by a meat dish, vegetables, and salad. For dessert there is usually a Polish pastry or fruit with cheese.

✳

Still, the Holy Father pays little attention to what is on his plate. He's more interested in the lunch-table

The pope with religious leaders during his travels

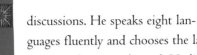

discussions. He speaks eight languages fluently and chooses the language spoken at each meal. He listens intently and takes notes, often leaving his plate untouched.

After lunch, the once active, mountaineering pontiff takes a half-hour nap at the insistence of his doctors. Then he relaxes on his rooftop terrace in an hour of meditation and prayer. Until supper, at about 7:30

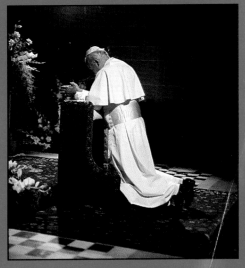

Prayer, more than food or drink, sustains the pope

P.M., he works in his office.

The pope's dinner companions are usually friends. On Fridays he has a standing date with Joseph Cardinal Ratzinger, prefect of the Congregation for the Doctrine of the Faith. They became friends at the Second Vatican Council. On Saturday evenings he meets with Bernardin Cardinal Gantin, who heads the Vatican's congregation for bishops. During this meal a frequent topic of

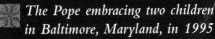

*The Pope embracing two children
in Baltimore, Maryland, in 1995*

discussion is the naming of new
bishops.

※

For the balance of the evening, John
Paul prepares for the next day's audiences in his private study. He also
spends time brushing up on languages of which he does not yet have
full command. Between 10:45 and
midnight, the pope ends his day with
prayers and meditation before allow-
ing himself a well-deserved rest.

Peace Traveler

John Paul II is the most traveled pope in history. He has visited more than 100 countries, championing the oppressed and bringing hope and enlightenment to people all over the globe.

In January 1979, when he visited Mexico on his first papal visit outside Italy, his holiness deplaned, knelt, and kissed the ground, a gesture that would become the trademark of papal visits for many years.

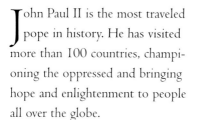

The pope kissing Spanish soil upon his arrival at Madrid Airport

Since recovering from hip replacement surgery in 1995, he is now offered a bowl of soil of the country he is visiting on which to plant the papal kiss.

※

John Paul traveled to Poland in June 1979. His election and his visit helped to unite Polish Catholics with Catholics around the world. Eventually the solidarity of the Poles and the pope's resolute stand against communism would help to defeat the

 The pope walking through the Hill of Crosses in Lithuania

Communist system throughout eastern Europe.

John Paul visited Brazil in June of 1980, where he asserted the right of Brazilian workers to form trade unions. In Portugal, during May 1982, he urged the Portuguese government to allow peasants to work their own land.

On a trip to Canada in September 1984, he admonished the rich of

The pope with former President and Nancy Reagan

North America for excessive materialism and political supremacy at the expense of their poorer neighbors to the south. When he visited the United States the following fall, he addressed his concern about America's lack of commitment to moral truth: "Every generation of Americans needs to know that freedom consists not in doing what we like but in having the right to do what we ought."

The pope at the United Nations in
October 1995

In May 1996 he traveled to Colombia and again targeted the wealthy and implored them to "shed their spiritual blindness." When he made the first-ever papal visit to Lebanon in May 1977, he urged peace: "Violence will never triumph over dialogue, nor fear and caution over confidence, nor hatred over fraternal love."

Pope John Paul traveled to Cuba in January 1998. He hoped to normal-

 Fidel Castro greeting the pope on his historic visit to Cuba

ize church-state relations, but he also denounced Cuba's denial of human rights. Next he took the United States to task for the economic embargo imposed upon the Cuban people since 1962 and urged America "to change, to change."

John Paul II has made nine visits to Africa, where he appeared to especially enjoy the colorful and joyous receptions he has been given. He has traveled to Australia, Fiji, and Singa-

pore. But it was right in St. Peter's
Square on a spring afternoon in
1981 that an attempt was made on
his life—an attempt that almost suc-
ceeded. Somehow, John Paul sur-
vived, and just a few days later he
asked that his would-be assassin be
forgiven. Before long he was traveling
again, speaking out against injustice
and working tirelessly for a world in
which peace and human dignity
could flourish.

In John Paul's
Words

*B*ut no darkness of error or of sin can totally take away from man the light of God the Creator.

—Encyclical *Veritatis Splendor*,
August 6, 1993

※

*N*ew knowledge leads us to recognize the theory of evolution as [more] than a hypothesis.

—Message to the Pontifical Acade-
my of Sciences, October 1996, as
reported in *Skeptical Inquirer*,
January–February 1997

Totus tuus.

—John Paul's motto, which means "I am wholly yours," or "All thine."

※

People's ideas, activities, and under-takings—however commonplace they may be—are used by the Creator to renew the world, to lead it to salvation, to make it a more perfect instrument of divine glory.

—"The Church Must Learn to Cope with the Computer Culture," World Communications Day, May 27, 1989

*S*uffering seems to belong to man's transcendence: It is one of those points in which man is in a certain sense "destined" to go beyond himself, and he is called to this in a mysterious way.

—Apostolic letter *Salvifici Doloris,*
February 11, 1984

In you there is hope, for you belong to the future, just as the future belongs to you.

Apostolic letter *Dilecti Amici,* March 31,
1985, for International Youth Year

79

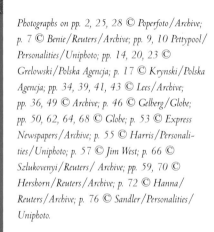